Camp Toccoa

First Home of the Airborne
1942-1944

G.G. Stokes, Jr.

Dedication

This book is dedicated to the Paratroopers who trained to serve this country at Camp Toccoa, Georgia during the dark and uncertain days of World War II.

And

The members of the Stephens County Historical Society who keep their memories alive.

Acknowledgment

Special thanks to Nadene Carter of Norlights Press, Inc. for her help in the technical aspects of this project.

Visit the Author's Website

www.GeorgiaWriter.com

Camp Toccoa:
First Home of the Airborne
1942-1944
G.G. Stokes, Jr.

Originally intended as a training area for Georgia State Guard[1] units as large as a division, construction on what was to become Camp Toccoa began in 1938. The U.S. Forest Service purchased the 17,000 acres of rough, mountainous terrain on and around Currahee Mountain in Northeast Georgia[2] for one dollar per acre[3] and, early in 1942, it was selected as the training site for the Army's new Parachute Infantry units. It was there that volunteers completed their processing and basic training before being sent to bases such as Fort Benning, Georgia to complete their airborne training.[4] The *Toccoa Record* first announced the expansion of Camp Robert Toombs in its July 16, 1942, edition, reporting that the Paratroopers were to be "college men" who would receive salaries based on pay for paratroopers.[5] Jump pay was $50 per month,[6] a sizable bonus that doubled the pay of an Army private.[7] Within a few weeks of Camp Toombs' activation as a federal military installation, the Louise Hotel, located on Lake Louise to the east of Toccoa, was taken over and converted into the camp's hospital. The hospital, complete with a staff of doctors, nurses, and their quarters was commanded throughout its existence by Col. G.G. Woodruff.[8]

Unlike the hospital at Lake Louise, leadership at Camp Toccoa changed often. In the first few months of its existence the base had four separate commanders. The first was Colonel J.O. Tarbox, who served until August 12, 1942 when he was replaced by Col. L.L. Berry.[9] Col. Berry commanded for only two months before turning over the leadership of the post to Lt. Col. Frank T. Addington in October 1942.[10] Colonel Addington was, in turn, replaced by Col. Patrick J. Hurley in May 1943.[11]

The name, Camp Robert Toombs, was one of the first casualties of the new training area. Having to de-train at the Toccoa railroad depot and travel on Highway 13 past the Toccoa Casket Company to Camp Toombs[12] sounded somewhat foreboding. At the request of the troops, the name of the camp was officially changed to Camp Toccoa on August 19, 1942.[13]

Other than the construction of a rifle range, no major construction had been undertaken prior to the camp being transferred to federal authority.[14] Tents, or hutments, that held fifteen men each, were originally used for both officers and enlisted personnel.[15] The tents were eventually replaced by barracks moved from an abandoned Civilian Conservation Corps camp near Royston, Georgia.[16] Later additions included an amphitheater, which was constructed for USO shows and bi-weekly movies, and a post office run by military personnel, which opened on the base at the end of 1942.[17] By January 1943, Camp Toccoa also contained a base chapel, service club, movie theater,[18] cafeteria, auditorium, and a bowling alley, along with several post exchanges and other recreational facilities.[19] An Officer's Club established at the Woodford Place on the highway near the camp was known as the 506th Parachute Infantry Officer's Club.

To ferry the troops between the town and the camp, a bus service was instituted which the soldiers could use day or night.[20] Popular destinations in Toccoa included the Ritz

Theater, the USO building, and the municipal swimming pool.[21] Other recreation areas were Lake Louise and Toccoa Falls College.[22]

Five parachute regiments trained at Camp Toccoa between 1942 and 1944. The first was the 506th Parachute Infantry Regiment, which was activated there on July 20, 1942. The men of the 506th are remembered by their unique battle cry. Instead of the more commonly used "Geronimo!" they would shout "Currahee!"[23] as they jumped. This would make them famous as the "Currahee Regiment."[24] One colorful group dubbed "The Flying Thirteen" trained with the 506th during the summer of 1942. The Flying Thirteen consisted of Cherokee and Yaqui Indians, a Hindu high diver, a number of former dare-devil automobile drivers, and several college athletes.[25]

The 501st Parachute Infantry Regiment, activated on November 15, 1942, followed the 506th at Camp Toccoa. On January 5, 1943, the 511th Parachute Infantry Regiment and the 457th Parachute Field Artillery Battalion were activated. The last regiment to train at Camp Toccoa was the 517th Parachute Infantry Regiment, activated on March 15, 1943. All of these regiments, with the exception of the 511th Parachute Infantry, were attached to the 101st Airborne Division and served in the European Theater of Operations. The 511th was assigned to the 11th Airborne Division and served in the Pacific Theater.[26] Other units that served at Camp Toccoa were the 38th Signal Construction Battalion and the 305th Signal Operations Battalion.[27]

Although Camp Toccoa was a training base for airborne troops, very few actual jumps took place there. The few that did used a cornfield on top of Dicks Hill, just across the county line in neighboring Habersham County as a drop zone.[28] Because of its short length, transport planes could barely take off and land safely on the base runway. When the wheels of a plane returning from a jump in Gainesville,

Georgia hit the soft shoulder of the runway, turning the plane on its side,[29] jumps at Camp Toccoa were ended. From that time on, they were confined to the camp's thirty-five foot jump tower that used a series of pulleys and cables to simulate conditions of an airborne descent.[30]

The training at Camp Toccoa was tough. Robert Ryals, who trained at Camp Toccoa, remembers that the would-be paratroopers ended up in one of two ways: "It made men out of them, or they went elsewhere."[31] Days started early; physical training was conducted by the regimental commander prior to breakfast and often included a run up Currahee Mountain. After breakfast the actual training commenced, often lasting more than fourteen hours a day. Evenings were spent in classroom instruction;[32] days were spent doing close order drill and calisthenics.[33] New Jersey Congressman, J. Pernell Thomas, a member of the House Military Affairs Committee who had a son serving as a private in the 501st Parachute Infantry, visited the camp in January of 1943. He noted that the officers and men of the camp took the daily routine of navigating the obstacle course and running up and down Currahee Mountain as "all in a day's work."[34]

The ritual of the Currahee Mountain run originated during the early days of the camp. Upon his arrival at Camp Toccoa, Pvt. Ed Tipper, a member of the 506th Parachute Infantry, looked up at the mountain and remarked to a comrade, "I'll bet that when we finish the training program here, the last thing they'll make us do is climb that mountain." His words proved to be swiftly prophetic when a few minutes later someone blew a whistle. The unit fell in and was ordered to change into boots and athletic trunks before beginning the first of many three-mile runs to the summit of Currahee and back.[35] Lt. John White of the 501st Parachute Infantry set the record time on the round trip run when he completed it in thirty-eight minutes.[36] Today, this tradition is continued by modern-day runners competing in the annual Currahee Challenge.

In addition to physical stress, the leaders of the 506th often added realism to the training. The troopers would never forget Thanksgiving Day 1942 when hog innards - hearts, livers, guts, and all - were strewn 18 inches below a maze of wire that they crawled through on their stomachs as machine gun bullets zipped over their heads.[37]

One regiment set two world records while training at Camp Toccoa. In October 1942, the 650 officers and men of the 506th Parachute Infantry marched in full field gear from Clemson College in South Carolina to Camp Toccoa, a distance of 42 miles in 18 hours and 10 minutes.[38] Then, between December 1st and 3rd 1942, the Second Battalion of the 506th made a record march of 100 miles from Toccoa to Atlanta, Georgia.[39]

This march was conducted after Col. Robert Sink, the commanding officer of the 506th, read a *Reader's Digest* article about a Japanese unit that set a world record by marching 100 miles down the Malayan Peninsula in 72 hours. He was certain that "his men" could do it better. Since the regiment was already scheduled to move to Fort Benning, Col. Sink sent the 1st and 3rd Battalions by train while the 2nd Battalion was selected to perform this feat of endurance. At 0700 hours on December 1, 1943, four companies set out from the flagpole at Camp Toccoa in full field gear. Their destination was Atlanta, Georgia 118 miles away by road. The weather was freezing cold, but, after enduring many hardships, they were able to set a new record by covering the distance in 33 hours and 3 minutes of actual marching time. Footsore, and in some cases being supported by their comrades, the battalion marched into Five Points in downtown Atlanta along a route that was lined with cheering spectators and bands. When Colonel Sink was asked to comment about the 12 men who failed to complete the march, he proudly replied, "When they fell out, they fell forward."[40]

Camp Toccoa may also have set another record by producing one of the youngest American Legion members of the war. In late 1942 one of the trainees, 15 year old Raymond L. Beeman of Pueblo, Colorado was found to be underage and was discharged for minority when the Army learned his true age. He left the camp with tears in his eyes, his dream of becoming a paratrooper at an end. After his discharge, Beeman returned home and became a member of American Legion Post No. 2.[41]

Such an intensive training program was not without mishaps. During 1943 at least four soldiers lost their lives while serving at Camp Toccoa. On February 9, 1943 a machine gun being disassembled for cleaning accidentally discharged, killing Private Martin J. Govednik of Joliet, Illinois. Private Govednik was a member of the 501st Parachute Infantry.[42] Only a few days later a second soldier, Private Paul Magna, was killed while on maneuvers near Ayersville, Georgia when he was struck and instantly killed by a train.[43] Four months later, on June 5, 1943 during an unusual heat wave that struck the area, a member of the 517th Parachute Infantry, Private Willard J. Johnson from Kanon Falls, Minnesota suffered a sunstroke and was taken to the camp hospital where he died the following morning.[44] A fourth man, Private Thomas B. Jones, a member of the cadre at Camp Toccoa, drowned in Lake Louise in September 1943. His body was recovered by the military on September 10, 1943.[45]

On May 30, 1943, news raced through Toccoa and the surrounding area that many of the men at the camp had died and many hundreds were hospitalized. The camp was besieged by telephone calls and visitors seeking to learn news of their husbands, sons, or friends. There had been no fatalities although 98 of the service men had been hospitalized due to a severe outbreak of food poisoning. All of those affected recovered and were released by the camp hospital at Lake Louise on the following Wednesday.[46]

Although the camp was almost exclusively a male domain, there were a handful of women present. Other than the wives of the officers and enlisted men, and the Army nurses assigned to the base hospital, female civilians worked on post. Interestingly, the first "women in uniform" were not military, but civilian employees of the camp who decided in early 1943 to initiate their own uniforms as a symbol of their patriotism.[47] After agreeing on a military-style cut, they chose blue as the color for their uniforms.[48] A blue garrison cap topped off the ensemble.[49] The first female military personnel who were not Army nurses arrived on August 13, 1943 in the persons of Lt. Emily Cannon and Lt. Kathleen Good. Both WAC's (Women's Army Corps) assumed duties as operational officers and were quartered with the nurses at the post hospital.[50]

As in many World War II movies, there were weddings between the soldiers and local girls. Some of the soldiers even returned to Toccoa after the war and made it their home. Others brought their sweethearts with them and married them on post. The marriage of Pvt. Theodore E. Dziepak and Miss Betty Weir, both of Perth Amboy, N.J., was presided over by the post chaplain, John S. Maloney. It took place on October 28, 1942 and may have been the first performed on the base.[51] Many of these wives lived in rented rooms in the town.[52]

On February 3, 1943, the Enlisted Men's Wives Club, located in the former Women's Club of Toccoa,[53] held its first meeting with Mrs. Lloyd Baker of Indianapolis, Indiana acting as the temporary chairperson.[54] The club aided in the war effort by making surgical dressings and participating in other Red Cross work.[55] The feminine hand was also felt in other ways throughout the base. In early 1943, Mrs. Mary Smith headed members of the Toccoa Pilot Club in refurbishing and decorating a lounge for the troops. Originally, it had been nothing more than a spacious room containing three stoves and a radio. After applying ingenuity, time, and some good-old-fashioned *elbow grease*, the members of the Pilot Club transformed it into a gaily decorated room with burgundy curtains, deep comfortable chairs, desks, writing paper, tables, softly shaded lamps, ash trays, magazine racks, magazines, cards, and games.[56] One soldier, Edward J. Gulewiez, summed up their fondness for the actions of one woman, Mrs. Alva Willgus, the wife of the local U.S.O. director, in a farewell letter published in the *Toccoa Record* on May 4, 1942. "To Mrs. Alva Willgus, who is known to all the boys as Mom… we shall never forget you… for you have been our mom during our stay here in Toccoa… with tears in my eyes, I bid, farewell."[57]

Although patriotism was at an all-time high during the Second World War, and many residents of Toccoa and Stephens County went out of the way to welcome the soldiers, friction developed between the troops and some of the townspeople. In an anonymous letter to the editor of the *Toccoa Record* on Nov. 12, 1942, a soldier claimed that the theater had been closed on Sundays in order to keep the soldiers out.[58] It was commonly thought that one prominent local man, Reverend R.A. Forrest, the founder and president of Toccoa Falls College, was the instigator of the theater closing because he did not approve of the military base being located in Stephens County. His reasons for this stance were that there were several "beer joints," notably the Tadpole Inn[59] and the Hi-de-ho, which were located just outside the camp's gate,[60] and that people should rest on Sundays and not go to the theater. This would indicate that he had nothing against the soldiers themselves, only the unchristian influences that seemed to follow army bases in general.[61] In an open letter to the newspaper on Dec. 10, 1942, Reverend Forrest rebutted the accusation that the theaters were closed in order to keep the soldiers out. He explains that although it was actually a violation of Georgia State law for them to be opened on Sundays, they were allowed to operate solely for the soldiers. He claimed that attendance was so low, the theater could not make money and that was the actual reason why it had been closed.[62]

Not withstanding, the people of the surrounding area generally welcomed the soldiers. "They thought quite a bit of us, although we were wild. Well, the country was wild then," remembers Albert Beasley who served in both the 506th and 517th Parachute Infantry during their training at Camp Toccoa.[63] Army officers were guests of the Kiwanis Club,[64] Lions Club,[65] and the Pilot club.[66] The Toccoa High School Band also did its part by performing for the troops at Camp Toccoa.[67] Soldiers were entertained in the homes of local citizens during the Christmas season[68] and local ladies entertained the troops at the camp hospital during the holidays.[69] The local Girl's Service Organization, a volunteer organization of women between the ages of 18 and 35, visited the camp and provided dancing partners for the troops.[70] Soldiers returned the compliment in such ways as providing entertainment with their ten-piece orchestra made up of musicians from the base,[71] opening the base to spectators for regimental reviews,[72] and marching in the local parades.[73]

Several bands were formed at the camp. Colonel Howard R. Johnston, the commander of the 501st Parachute Infantry, wanted an orchestra and a band for his regiment as a morale booster for the men. He selected Sergeant Philip Kirschner as the man to start it. The soldiers had no instruments at the time. The ones who had them at home sent for them, others were borrowed, and for the remainder, they took up a collection to buy them. After much hard work, the 501st Parachute Infantry Band had their debut at the Ritz Theater in Toccoa on Jan. 15, 1943, receiving rave reviews from the local press.[74]

Another band, dubbed the Second Army Ground Forces Dance Orchestra, under the direction of Corporal Dick Alexander, was also formed at Camp Toccoa. Many of its members had been musicians in civilian life, playing with bands such as those of Al Donahue, Dick Stabile, Carl Hoff, Louis Prima, and Reggie Childs.[75] Both of these groups did their part in keeping the morale of the local people and troops soaring. They performed everywhere from the Ritz Theater, to the courthouse lawn,[76] to the local sporting events. Sometimes they played together, sometimes separately. Eventually, the two groups merged into the Camp Toccoa Concert Band[77] consisting of over seventy musicians.[78] The camp had its own radio program that highlighted these talented musicians. "Thirty Minutes From Camp Toccoa" could be heard on the local station, WRLC, every Wednesday evening at 6:30 and Saturday afternoon at 1:30.[79] The names of the radio programs changed as units rotated through the camp. "At Ease," another show that originated at Camp Toccoa in 1943, featured the music of the Second Army Ground Forces Band.[80]

Although generally well-treated, many of the troops had mixed feelings about their stay at Camp Toccoa. Gerald Stokes, Sr. who served in the 517th in Europe, but did not train with them at Toccoa, remembers that many of the troops spoke of Toccoa as "hot and out in the middle of nowhere."[81]

Other than inspection tours by such high ranking officers as Brigadier General E.G. Chapman, the Commanding General of the Airborne command,[82] Camp Toccoa had its share of famous visitors. Bob Hope visited the camp on May 19, 1943, accompanied by entertainers such as Francis Langford, Vera Vague, and comic Jerry Colonna from his Pepsodent Radio Show. Hope and his entertainers began their performance late, after having first entertained in the officer's mess of the 517th Parachute Infantry. Hope's apology was accepted by the troops after he performed the time-honored punishment for a mistake in the armed forces, a half dozen pushups.[83] The troops loved him and applauded his performance as enthusiastically as they had applauded the entrance of the Army nurses from the station hospital prior to the show.

Camp Toccoa's contribution to the war effort was recognized when a feature article, complete with photographs, appeared in the April 1943 issue of the *U.S. Army Review*. The article, written to highlight the activities of the Parachute Infantry at the camp, was an immediate hit with the troops.[84]

The community also aided the war effort. Several issues of the *Toccoa Record* urged people to recycle by bringing scrap metal to the Camp Toccoa Quartermaster which was located in the old Swifts Fertilizer plant on Broad Street.[85]

Camp Toccoa was short-lived. Even as the war continued in Europe, it was returned to the State of Georgia on Oct. 1, 1944. Plans for its future use were that it would begin to house National Guard troops again while a portion of it would be used to house 250 to 300 "delinquents" who were in state care.[86] Approximately five million dollars had been spent to improve and operate the camp during the years of federal use.[87] The local community made an unsuccessful attempt to keep the camp open,[88] but by 1945 the transition was complete and Georgia Guard troops were again using the area for maneuvers and target practice.[89]

Most of Camp Toccoa has disappeared with time, yet its legacy lingers in tales told by those who served there and by the old timers of the area. One humorous story is found in Gerald Astor's book, *Battling Buzzards*. The 517th lacked a mascot and one of its members, Lt. John "Tiger" Rohr, prevailed upon the St. Louis Zoo to provide a lion cub to the First Battalion. The animal proved to be something of a nuisance, shredding mattresses and pillows and abusing its handlers. Still, Col. Walsh tolerated it because of the boost it gave to the unit's morale. This changed when a group of officers decided to drive into town for a celebration party. Someone thought the mascot should accompany them and it, apparently like all felines, did not ride well. The cub swung his paw in the car, raking Major William J. Boyle, the 1st Battalion commander, across the head. The following morning Boyle arrived at the rifle range with his "steel helmet perched high upon a turban-like bandage." Soon afterward, the mascot was given to the 515th Parachute Infantry as a gift.[90]

According to another story, the family of one Eastonollee, Georgia. resident, Lee Howard, farmed the area near Camp Toccoa. They had a small dog that began to stray onto the post. Soldiers, who are notorious for befriending stray animals, began to feed the dog. During road marches past the farm, the dog would run out to welcome the soldiers as they passed. When the unit completed its training, it asked for the dog as a mascot. It accompanied the unit to Europe and the soldiers returned the family's favor by sending photographs of themselves and the dog to the family.[91]

Another Toccoa resident, Mr. Lamar Davis, remembers that as a child during that time period "you could not come to town on a Friday or Saturday night without seeing the streets and depot filled with soldiers." Fights were frequent in the downtown establishments, with people sometimes being thrown through plate glass windows. One establishment put itself "off limits" to soldiers because of the damage it repeatedly sustained during these altercations. Another incident that Mr. Davis "will never forget" was the sight of Camp Toccoa soldiers marching on the football field of Eastanollee school. To a young boy raised in what was then an isolated area of Northeast Georgia, the military band and large numbers of people was a memorable event.[92]

The presence of the soldiers had a positive impact on the economy of the area. During its first year, the payroll for the troops exceeded $2,000,000 and the civilian payroll was $600,000.[93] Over 18,000 troops passed through the camp, a fact that one entrepreneurial Toccoa resident, Henry Powers, turned into cash. Selling ham sandwiches to the soldiers at the Toccoa Railroad Depot, he would check the arrival and departure schedules and be waiting when the trains arrived, in some cases selling sandwiches through the open windows of the passenger cars.[94]

During the dedication of the Camp Toccoa monument in 1990, a fifty-year-old mystery was solved. Mrs. Mildred Carroll of Eastanollee, Georgia., who was attending the ceremony, asked veterans of the 517th Parachute Infantry if they had known a member of the unit named Paul Blasko. The faces of the veterans changed immediately and she was told, "we don't ever mention that name." They informed her that Paul Blasko had been a deserter from the regiment. But was he? No one knew better than Mrs. Carroll.

Mrs. Carroll met and married Paul Blasko when he was training at Camp Toccoa. He was a good soldier, a sergeant in the 517th Parachute Infantry who loved "his boys." Often, when Paul and Mildred were in town together, they would see the men from his unit and he would point proudly and exclaim, "there are my boys!" After his training, she moved with him to Camp Mackall, North Carolina. She returned home, but came back to visit when the unit's deployment to Europe grew near. She was young and when it was time to return to Toccoa, she was so upset that Paul went with her to the bus station in Charlotte. He told her that he would take her as far as Charlotte, but then he must go directly back to camp. At the station, Paul was approached by the Military Police who asked him, "aren't you supposed to be in camp?" Paul admitted that he was, but that he was simply seeing his wife off and that he was "fixing to go back." The Military Police told him that he would have to go with them, and he asked if he could see Mildred off before he went. They agreed and waited until she was gone before arresting him. During his several months in the stockade, Paul was not allowed to write Mildred, but when her mother passed away he was able to smuggle out a note expressing his sorrow. After he was released, he was placed in the 513th Parachute Infantry and sent to Europe.

Like all soldiers, he had formed a close bond with his comrades. In a letter he wrote to Mildred, he said, "I thought that maybe I would run into some of the guys that I was with at Camp Mackall. These are a pretty good bunch of boys, but they're not like the ones that I trained with." On January 7, 1945, Paul G. Blasko was wounded at Bastogne, Belgium during the Battle of the Bulge. He died three days later on Jan. 10, 1945. The Toccoa Record announced his death on March 8, 1945.[95] When Mildred asked a fellow soldier how he died, all that he would say was that, "It was so bad over there, you wouldn't want to know what it was like." When one of his old officers from the 517th heard the story at the reunion, he was relieved. "All these years I have thought about him and wondered what happened. I really, really trusted that guy." He admitted that, "in similar circumstances I would have done the same thing." For over fifty years the men of the 517th considered him a deserter, and they had never known his fate. That day, Paul G. Blasko was reunited with "his boys".[96]

Little remains of Camp Toccoa. With its deactivation, barracks were moved or demolished, and the property was eventually turned into an industrial park. Only three of the structures remain on their original sites: a small block building now used by the Milliken Plant, a water tank which still stands on the hill behind Patterson Pump Company, and the water works constructed by the US Army and later bought by the city of Toccoa. One building moved from the camp served as a sanctuary for the nearby Welcome Home Baptist Church until it burned.[97]

A monument was erected by the Stephens County Historical Society on November 18, 1990[98] at what was once the entrance to Camp Toccoa. It occupies a concrete pad which in the heyday of the camp contained a vintage World War I tank.[99] The monument commemorates the bravery and sacrifice of those who trained to serve their country in the shadow of Currahee Mountain during the dark and uncertain days of World War II.

Works Cited

Allen, Mitchell, eyewitness, interview by author, Toccoa, Ga., 1 Aug. 1998.

Ambrose, Stephen E. *Band of Brothers: E Company 506th Regiment, 101st Airborne, From Normany to Hitler's Eagles Nest*, NYC: Simon and Schoster, 1996.

Astor, Gerald. *Battling Buzzards: The Odyssey of the 517th Parachute Regimental Combat Team. 1943-45* NYC: Donald I. Fine, Inc., 1993.

Beasley, Albert, member of 506th and 517th Parachute Infantry, interview by author, telephone, Toccoa Ga., 18 July 1998.

Carroll, Mildred, eyewitness, interview by author, telephone, Eastanollee, Ga., 19 July 1998.

Davis, Lamar, local historian and eyewitness, interview by author, Toccoa, Ga., 11,14 July 1998.

Howard, Arthur Lee, local resident and eyewitness, interview by author, telephone, Eastanollee, Ga., 18 July 1998.

Neal, Patrick. "Camp Toccoa Survivor Looks Back on Paratroop Days." *Chieftain and Toccoa Record* 18 June 1996. 2(A).

Pruitt, Kim, Stephens County Historical Society, interview by author, Toccoa, Ga., 20 June 1998.

Ryles, Robert, member of 501st Parachute Infantry, interview by author, telephone, Southern Pines, North Carolina, 6 July 1998.

Stevens County Georgia and its People. Vol 1. Waynesville, North Carolina: Walsworth Pub., 1996.

Stokes, Gerald G. Sr., member of 517th Parachute Infantry Regimental Combat Team, interview by author, Americus, Ga., 1 July 1998.

Toccoa Record. 16, 23 July; 6,20,27 August; 6 September; 15, 29 October; 5, 12, 19 November; 10,17, 31 December; 1942; 7, 14, 21, 28 January; 4, 11, 18, 25 February; 4, 11, 18, 25 March; 1, 22 April; 20 May; 3, 10 June; 15 July; 19 August; 9, 23 September; ·1943; 24 May; 15 June; 14 September; 1944; 1, 8 March 1945.

Other Books by G.G. Stokes, Jr.

Nonfiction

Camp Toccoa:
First Home of the Airborne.
1942-1944

Historical Fiction

Letters For Catherine:
A Novel of Charleston
During the American Revolution

A Lesser Form of Patriotism:
A Novel of the King's Carolina Rangers and
the American Revolution in the South.

Loving Lynn Celia:
A Novel of the
French and Indian War in the South

The Road to Bloody Marsh:
A Novel of King George's War

Endnotes

1. "Camp Toombs Being Readied to Accommodate 2,000 Soldiers During Next Six Weeks, Says War Dept.," Toccoa Record, 16 July 1942, p. l.
2. Currahee Mountain is located approximately three miles east of the town of Toccoa, Ga.
3. Stephens County Georgia and Its People, vol. 1, Stephens County Historical Society, Inc., and Don Mills, Inc., (Waynesville, N.C.: Walsworth Pub., 1996), 48-49
4. Ibid
5. "Camp Toombs Being Readied to Accommodate 2,000 Soldiers During Next Six Weeks, Says War Dept.," Toccoa Record, 16 July 1942, p.1.
6. Stephens County Georgia and Its People, vol. 1, Stephens County Historical Society, Inc., and Don Mills, Inc., (Waynesville, N.C.: Walsworth Pub., 1996), 49
7. "An eye to the Sky," Toccoa Record, 4 March 1943, p. 1.
8. "Camp Toccoa Celebrates First Anniversary July 14th; 18,000 Troops Stationed Here During the Year. With Payroll in Excess of $2,000,000; Civilian Payroll $600,000 Year." Toccoa Record, 15 July 1943, p.1.
9. "Col. Tarbox Leaves for New Post Amid Intense Activity at Camp Toccoa." Toccoa Record, 20 August 1942, p.1.
10. "Lt. Col. Frank Addington Succeeds Col. L.L. Berry as Camp Commander" Toccoa Record, 15 October 1942, p.1.
11. "Camp Toccoa Celebrates First Anniversary July 14th; 18,000 Troops Stationed Here During Year. With Payroll in Excess of $2,000,000; Civilian Payroll $600,000 Year," Toccoa Record, 15 July 1943, p.1.
12. Mrs. Kim Pruitt, Stephens County Historical Society, interview by author, Toccoa, Georgia, 20 June 1998.
13. "Col. Tarbox Leaves for, New Post Amid Intense Activity at Camp Toccoa," Toccoa Record, 20 August 1942, p. 1.
14. Stephens County Georgia and Its People, vol. 1, Stephens County Historical Society, Inc., and Don Mills, Inc., (Waynesville, N.C.: Walsworth Pub., 1996), 48-49

15 "Troops Arriving," Toccoa Record, 6 August 1942, p.1.

16 Mrs. Kim Pruitt, Stephens County Historical Society, interview by author, Toccoa, Georgia, 20 June 1998

17 "Post Office at Camp Toccoa to Open in Near Future," Toccoa Record, 17 December 1942, p.1.

18 "New Post Chapel at Camp Toccoa to be Dedicated," Toccoa Record, 21 January 1942, p.1.

19 "Camp Toccoa Celebrates First Anniversary July 14th; 18,000 Troops Stationed Here During Year. With Payroll in Excess of $2,000,000; Civilian Payroll $600,000 Year," Toccoa Record, 15 July 1943, p.1.

20 "Col. Tarbox Leaves for New Post Amid Intense Activity at Camp Toccoa." Toccoa Record, 20 August 1942, p.1.

21 "Camp Toccoa Celebrates First Anniversary July 14th; 18,000 Troops Stationed Here During Year. With Payroll in Excess of $2,000,000; Civilian Payroll $600,000 Year," Toccoa Record, 15 July 1943, p.1.

22 Forrest, R.A. "An Open Letter From Rev. R.A. Forrest," Toccoa Record, 10 December 1942, p. 1-5.

23 Stephens County Georgia and Its People, vol. 1, Stephens County Historical Society, Inc., and Don Mills, Inc., (Waynesville, N.C.: Walsworth Pub., 1996), 49

24 Davis Lamar, "Dedication Ceremony, Camp Toccoa Monument" Speech presented at the dedication of the Camp Toccoa Monument by Lamar, Davis, Toccoa, Georgia, November 18, 1990.

25 "Group Composed of Cherokee and Yaqui Redmen," Toccoa Record, 15 June 1943, p. 1.

26 Stephens County Georgia and its People. Vol. 1, Stephens County Historical Society Inc., and Don Mills, Inc., (Waynesville, NC. Walsworth Pub., 1996), p. 49

27 "Camp Toccoa Celebrates First Anniversary July 14th: 18,000 Troops Stationed Here During Year. With Payroll in Excess of $2,000,000: Civilian Payroll $600,000 Year," Toccoa Record, 15 July 1943, p. 1.

28 Mr. Albert Beasley, 506th and 517th Parachute Infantry Regiments, interview by author, telephone conversation, Toccoa, Georgia, 18 July 1998.

Camp Toccoa

29   Mr. Albert Beasley, 506th and 517th Parachute Infantry Regiments, interview by author, telephone conversation, Toccoa, Georgia, 18 July 1998.

30   Mr. Lamar Davis, interview by author, Toccoa, Georgia, 11 July 1998.

31   Neal, Patrick. "Camp Toccoa Survivor Looks Back on Paratroop Days," Chieftain and Toccoa Record, 18 June 1996, p.2A.

32   Mr. Robert Ryles, 501st Parachute Infantry Regiment, interview by author, telephone conversation, Southern Pines, North Carolina, 6 July 1998.

33   Mr. Albert Beasley, 506th and 517th Parachute Infantry Regiments, interview by author, telephone conversation, Toccoa, Georgia, 18 July 1998.

34   "Congressman Thomas Pleased With Conditions at Camp Toccoa: Praises Officers, Men," Toccoa Record, 21 January 1943. p.1.

35   Ambrose, Stephen E., Band of Brothers: E Company 506th Regiment, 101st Airborne, From Normandy to Hitler's Eagle Nest. (NY; Simon and Schoster, 1992), 16-17

36   "An Eye to the Sky," Toccoa Record, 10 March 1945, p. 1.

37   Ambrose, Stephen E., Band of Brothers: E Company 506th Regiment, 101st Airborne, From Normandy to Hitler's Eagle Nest. (NY; Simon and Schoster, 1992), 25

38   "Parachute Battalion Established Record by 42-Mile March," Toccoa Record, 29 October 1942, p. 1.

39   "506th Parachute Troops Move Out, 501st Coming In," Toccoa Record, 10 December 1942, p.1.

40   Ambrose, Stephen E., Band of Brothers: E Company 506th Regiment, 101st Airborne, From Normandy to Hitler's Eagle Nest. (NY; Simon and Schoster, 1992), 26-27

41   The Camp Reporter, "An Eye to the Sky," Toccoa Record, 11 March 1943, p.8.

42   "Soldier Dies at Camp Toccoa by Accidental Shot," Toccoa Record, 11 February 1943, p.1.

43   "An Eye to the Sky," Toccoa Record, 18 February 1943, p.5.

44   "Unusual Heat Wave Claims Life of 517th Parachute Inf. Soldier," Toccoa Record, 10 June 1943, p.1.

45 "Camp Toccoa Soldier Drowns in Lake Louise," Toccoa Record, 9 September 1943, p.1.

46 "Parachutists Recovering From Food Poisoning," Toccoa Record, 3 June 1943, p. 1.

47 The Camp Reporter (pseud.) "An Eye to the Sky," Toccoa Record, 25 March 1943, p.1.

48 "An eye to the Sky," Toccoa Record, 18 February 1943, p.8.

49 "Girls Don Uniforms at Camp Toccoa," Toccoa Record, 25 March 1943, p.1.

50 "Two WAC Officers at Camp Toccoa," Toccoa Record, 19 August 1943, p.1.

51 "Wedding at Camp Toccoa," Toccoa Record, 19 November 1942, p.4.

52 "Notice to Landlords," Toccoa Record, 25 February 1943, p.4.

53 "Toccoa USO Dedicatory Program is Scheduled for Easter Sunday," Toccoa Record, 22 April 1943, p.1.

54 "Enlisted Men's Wives Form Club in Toccoa," Toccoa Record, 4 February 1943, p. 4.

55 Ibid

56 "Toccoa Pilot Club Helps Soldiers Outfit Recreation Rooms Here," Toccoa Record, 18 February 1943, p.3.

57 Gulewiez, Edward J. "A Soldier Writes Farewell to Toccoa," Toccoa Record, 24 May 1944, p.2.

58 "A Soldier's Sunday," Toccoa Record, 12 November 1942, p. 1.

59 Mr. Mitchell Allen, eyewitness, interview by author, Toccoa, Ga. 1 Aug. 1998.

60 Mrs. Kim Pruitt, Stephens County Historical Society, interview by author, Toccoa, GA. 20 June 1998.

61 Ambrose, Stephen E., Band of Brothers: E Company 506th Regiment, 101st Airborne: From Normandy to Hitler's Eagle Nest. (NY: Simon and Schoster, 1992) p. 18. Ambrose states that: "the language was foul. The most commonly used word was the F-word. It substituted for adjectives, nouns, and verbs."

62 Forrest, R.A. "An Open Letter From Rev. R.A. Forrest," Toccoa Record, 10 Dec. 1942, p. 1-5.

63 Mr. Albert Beasley, 606th and 517th Parachute Infantry Regiments. Interview by author, Telephone conversation, Toccoa, Ga. 18 July 1998.

64   "Army Officers Guests Kiwanis Club Members Lake Rabun Tuesday," Toccoa Record, 23 July 1942, p. 1.

65   "Lions Club Members Pledge Blood Donations for Battlefield Use," Toccoa Record, 19 Aug. 1943, p.1.

66   Haugen, Orin D. LTC. "Headquarters 511th Parachute Infantry," Toccoa Record, 25 Feb. 1943, p.4.

67   "T.H.S. Band Plays For Soldiers at Camp Toccoa," Toccoa Record, 19 Nov. 1942, p. 1.

68   "Citizens Should Register for Holiday Soldier Guests," Toccoa Record, 17 Dec. 1942, p. 1.

69   Woodruff, Gerald G. LTC. "Col Woodruff Expresses Appreciation for Work done by Toccoa Ladies," Toccoa Record, 31 Dec. 1942, p. 1.

70   "G.S.O. to Entertain Soldiers Friday Night at U.S.O. Building," Toccoa Record, 7 Jan. 1943, p. 1.

71   "Camp Toccoa Orchestra Entertains Kiwanians; Judge Candler Speaks," Toccoa Record, 12 Nov. 1942, p. 1.

72   "An Eye to the Sky," Toccoa Record, 11 March 1943, p.1.

73   "Big Parade Scheduled in Toccoa to Celebrate Signing of 1918 Armistice," Toccoa Record, 5 Nov. 1942, p. 1.

74   "501st Parachute Band Wins Praise in First Program," Toccoa Record, 21 Jan. 1943, p. 1-3.

75   "Will Play at Bond Rally," Toccoa Record, 23 Sep. 1943, p. 1.

76   "501st Parachute Infantry Band to Give Concert Here Friday at 3:45 P.M.," Toccoa Record, 25 Feb. 1943, p. 1.

77   "Camp Toccoa Band Concert Pleases Large Audience Thursday Night," Toccoa Record, 18 March 1943, p. 1.

78   The Camp Reporter, "An Eye to the Sky," Toccoa Record, 11 March 1943, p. 1.

79   "An Eye to the Sky," Toccoa Record, 18 Feb. 1943, p. 8.

80   "Will Play at Bond Rally," Toccoa Record, 23 Sep. 1943, p. 1.

81   Mr. Gerald G. Stokes, Sr., 517th Parachute Infantry Regimental Combat Team, interview by author, Americus, Ga. 1 July 1998.

82   "It's Like This, General…" Toccoa Record, 14 Jan. 1943, p. 1.

83   "Bob Hope, Radio and Screen Comic, and party, Entertain Soldiers of Camp Toccoa Last Night," Toccoa Record, 20 May 1943, p. 1.

84   "An Eye to the Sky," Toccoa Record, 25 Feb. 1943, p. 5.

85   "Army Emergency Relief Drive at Camp Toccoa," Toccoa Record, 27 Aug. – 3 Sep. 1942, p. 1.

86   These "delinquents" were eventually moved to the old Tuberculosis hospital in Alto, Ga. Today it is Lee Arrendale State Prison.

87   "Camp Toccoa to be Returned to State by the United States on Oct. 1," Toccoa Record, 14 Sep. 1944, p. 1.

88   "Citizens Seek a Continuance of Camp Toccoa," Toccoa Record, 13 Jan. 1944, pg 1.

89   "5th Battalion of Ga. State Guard Troops Participate in Maneuvers and Target Practice at Camp Toccoa," Toccoa Record, 1 March 1945, p. 1.

90   Astor, Gerald. Battling Buzzards: The Odyssey of the 517th Parachute Regimental Combat Team. 1943-45. (NY: Donald I. Fine, Inc., 1993), 13

91   Mr. Lamar Davis, interview by author, Toccoa, Ga., 11 July 1998.

92   Mr. Lamar Davis, interview by author, Toccoa, Ga., 11 July 1998.

93   "Camp Toccoa Celebrates First Anniversary July 14th; 18,000 Troops Stationed Here During Year. With Payroll in Excess of $2,000,000; Civilian Payroll $600,000 Year," Toccoa Record, 15 July 1943, p. 1.

94   Mr. Lamar Davis, interview by author, Toccoa, Ga., 11 July 1998.

95   "Sgt. Paul G. Blasko Killed in Luxembourg," Toccoa Record, 8 March 1945, p. 1.

96   Mrs. Mildred Carroll, interview by author, telephone, Eastanollee, Ga. 19 July 1998.

97   Mr. Lamar Davis, interview by author, Toccoa, Ga. 11 July 1998.

98   Stephens County Georgia and It's People, vol. 1, Stephens County Historical Society Inc., and Don Mills, Inc., (Waynesville, NC,: Walsworth Pub., 1996), 49.

99   Mr. Lamar Davis, interview by author, Toccoa, Ga., 11 July 1998.

Made in the USA
Charleston, SC
08 May 2011